What Time Do You Call This?

A Play by John Townsend

Series Editors: Steve Barlow and Steve Skidmore

Published by Heinemann Educational Publishers
Halley Court, Jordan Hill, Oxford OX2 8EJ
A division of Reed Educational and Professional Publishing Ltd

OXFORD MELBOURNE AUCKLAND
JOHANNESBURG BLANTYRE GABORONE
IBADAN PORTSMOUTH NH (USA) CHICAGO

© John Townsend, 2001
Original illustrations © Heinemann Educational Publishers 2001

All rights reserved. No part of this publication may be reproduced in any material form (including photocopying or storing it in any medium by electronic means and whether or not transiently or incidentally to some other use of this publication) without the prior written permission of the copyright owner, except in accordance with the provisions of the Copyright, Designs and Patents Act 1988 or under the terms of a licence issued by the Copyright Licensing Agency Ltd, 90 Tottenham Court Road, London W1P 9HE. Applications for the copyright owner's written permission to reproduce any part of this publication should be addressed in the first instance to the publisher.

First published 2001
05 04 03 02 01
10 9 8 7 6 5 4 3 2 1
ISBN 0 435 21298 2

Illustrations by Keith Page
Cover Design by Shireen Nathoo Design
Cover artwork by Janet Woolley
Designed by Artistix, Thame, Oxon
Printed and bound in Great Britain by Biddles Ltd

Tel: 01865 888058 www.heinemann.co.uk

Contents

Characters 4

Scene One 6

Scene Two 16

Scene Three 26

Characters

Dad is Bob Huntley. He is Gemma's father, and is waiting impatiently for her to come home.

Mum is Doreen Huntley. She is Gemma's mother, and much calmer than her husband.

Gran is Gemma and Jack's grandmother. She has a good sense of fun.

Jack is Gemma's brother. He is 14, and likes to annoy his father.

Gemma is Jack's sister. She is 16 and likes going out to clubs.

Wayne is Gemma's new boyfriend. He looks rough, but in fact he is likeable and kind to Gemma.

There are two rooms on the stage. The audience should see the action in both rooms in scenes 2 & 3.

Scene One

It is Friday night at ten past eleven in the Huntleys' sitting room. Dad walks up and down looking at the clock on the mantelpiece. Mum is ironing, Gran is in an armchair reading the paper, and Jack is stretched out on the sofa, watching TV.

DAD: One more minute. *(Looking at his watch and tapping it)* I said – one more minute.

MUM: *(Putting down the iron)* We heard you, dear.

DAD: I mean it this time.

JACK: That's what you said last time.

DAD: When?

MUM: A minute ago.

GRAN: There's a good film on TV soon.

MUM: There's a hole in your socks, Jack.

DAD: Am I the only one in this house who cares? The only one sick with worry?

MUM: You're the only one walking up and down wearing a track in the carpet.

JACK: We've gone through this before, Dad.

DAD: Then she should know better. I told her. You heard me tell her.

JACK: The whole street heard you.

DAD: Not a minute past eleven o'clock. That's what I said.

MUM: She's sixteen, Bob.

DAD: And look at the time now.

GRAN: Ten past. The film starts in ten minutes.

JACK: *(Winking)* It's a bit late for you, isn't it, Gran? Past your bed time!

GRAN: Not when there's a good film on.

JACK: It's a bit late. It might be a bit strong for you.

GRAN: Let's hope so, dear!

DAD: She's gone against my word.

JACK: Don't worry about it, Dad.

DAD: Don't worry about it? Don't worry about it? That's the problem with young people today. You don't like doing as you're told.

GRAN: You sound just like your father, dear.

DAD: Does no one care about her? She's just sixteen. I told her to be back no later than eleven. She will have to be told.

MUM: Told what, love?

DAD: Told about rules of this house. She'll get a piece of my mind.

JACK: Oh, heck.

GRAN: You haven't got many pieces left!

DAD: Mum, this is not a joking matter. She's out there in a dangerous world.

MUM: Dangerous world? She's only gone to Tramps. It's a nightclub, not a den of sin.

DAD: That's what she tells you. And now she's twelve minutes late.

JACK: Wow! The sin of the century!

DAD: And you should be in bed, too.

JACK: Don't talk daft, Dad – it's Friday night. I never go to bed before midnight on a Friday. I look after Gran when she's watching her late night films.

GRAN: We like our bit of horror, don't we?

MUM: We've got our own bit of horror tonight, eh?

DAD: I keep telling you this is not funny. Kids today need to be told. Jack needs his sleep.

JACK: Not as much as you, Dad. I don't fall asleep each night in that chair!

GRAN: Ooh Jack, you do make me laugh.

DAD: Laugh? Laugh? Is that what you'll all be doing when the police ring? When I have to go down and see her lying on the slab.

MUM: I think you're being a bit over the top, Bob.

DAD: They said the same to the father of Jack The Ripper's victims.

GRAN: It was a far more dangerous world then.

DAD: Rubbish! Kids today have more to fear.

MUM: Like fathers who go up the wall when they come in a few minutes late.

DAD: A few minutes? A few minutes? Look at the time now.

JACK: Didn't you stay out late as a lad, Dad?

DAD: That's got nothing to do with it.

GRAN: I could tell stories about your dad, Jack.

MUM: So could I!

JACK: Bit of a one for the girls, eh, Dad?

DAD: Not when I was your age. I knew nothing about the birds and the bees then. I told you when you were ten. Remember?

JACK: I remember you went bright red.

DAD: Well you asked, so I told you.

JACK: What did I ask?

DAD: You asked me where you came from. So I sat you down, took a deep breath and told you the facts of life.

JACK: I only wanted to know if I came from Ipswich. You gave me a lecture about dogs and puppies. For years I thought I was a red setter! Anyway, I bet you used to go to parties, Dad.

GRAN: I once had to fetch him and carry him home.

DAD: I was tired.

GRAN: You were so drunk you ran upstairs and took all your clothes off to get into bed.

DAD: Very wise if you ask me.

GRAN: Not really. We were still on the bus!

DAD: We're not talking about me. Gemma's a girl.

JACK: True, and dressed to kill! I was the only one here when she left – looking real glam!

MUM: *(Firmly)* Jack, stop it.

DAD: *(Worried)* What did she look like?

MUM: Don't make it worse, Jack.

DAD: No, come on – I need to know. Jack, tell me. What did she look like?

JACK: Very nice skirt. Tight and short. High heels. Bright red, I think. Bare shoulders. Black tights.

DAD: What! My daughter dressed like that?

JACK: Her boyfriend looked a sight, too.

MUM: *(Cross)* Jack, cut it out.

DAD: Boyfriend? What boyfriend?

JACK: Wayne. Ten studs in his nose. Eyebrows shaved. And a tattoo of Elvis on his tongue. Cool!

MUM: He's a nice lad, Bob.

DAD: You knew? You knew she was going out half naked with a ... yob? You let her go?

MUM: They make a nice couple. Just good friends.

DAD: Good friends? Nice couple? That's what they said about Romeo and Juliet. And look at the mess they got into.

JACK: Wayne's no Romeo. He doesn't wear tights. At least, I don't think so!

GRAN: But what about some of the odd girls you brought home, Bob?

MUM: Really? I didn't know about this.

DAD: Before I met you. Anyway, it was different then. I was a boy. I knew how to look after myself.

GRAN: Ha! What about that Lucy Potter? She ate you alive.

JACK: Ooh, tell me more, Gran. Anyway, you're often late home yourself, Dad.

DAD: Never. I'm always on time. But just look at that clock now. This is beyond a joke.

JACK: You were late tonight. I was sitting here all by myself. Home alone!

DAD: *(Snapping)* You knew we'd gone shopping.

JACK: I could have been worried sick. Just a poor young lad left to look after himself.

MUM: When we got back you didn't even hear us with those headphones on.

DAD: And we weren't out all night at a rave in a skimpy outfit with a monster called Wayne.

GRAN: *(Winking)* No, but Tesco's was a bit on the wild side for my liking!

DAD: Why do you all make fun of me? No wonder the world is falling apart these days. No one cares any more.

JACK: Wayne will take care of her. His last girlfriend is still alive – just! They say the studs on his tongue got caught on her tooth-brace so the fire brigade had to cut them apart!

DAD: This is the last time. She's already on her last warning. From now on she's grounded. Why can't she go out with a smart lad?

GRAN: Like the son of your boss, dear?

DAD: Yes. He's smart. Clean and tidy. Malcolm is well brought up. He'd be good for Gemma.

MUM: Sshh!

JACK: What's the matter, Mum?

MUM: I think I heard the gate.

DAD: *(Rushing to the curtains to peep out)* I can't see anything. It's pitch black out there.

GRAN: I hope she's got a key.

DAD: Of course not. She'll have to ring the bell. I locked the back door. I've got the key.

JACK: I think I heard footsteps.

DAD: Then it's time for some harsh words.

MUM: It's only quarter past eleven. Don't go mad.

DAD: I'll go as mad as I like. She needs telling.

GRAN: It's gone very quiet.

JACK: The lull before the storm.

DAD: It's no good. I'm not going to wait any longer. I'm going to open that front door.

(Blackout.)

Scene Two

> The Huntleys' kitchen, a few minutes later. Mum is washing some cups at the sink while Dad walks up and down the kitchen.

MUM: I bet you feel silly.

DAD: *(Even more worked up)* If she doesn't walk through that door by the time this kettle's boiled, I'm going to make a phone call.

MUM: You made a proper fool of yourself.

DAD: It's warming up. Look – there's some steam.

MUM: That's what kettles are for. Now calm down.

DAD: It's stress. I can't think straight.

MUM: You made that quite clear just now. Poor woman.

DAD: It can't be helped. I had to open that front door and speak my mind.

MUM: Not to next door's cat. Poor Mrs Simpson nearly died of shock. She only crept round to get Fluffy when you burst open the door to shout, 'Get up to your room, I'll deal with you later.' She fell in the roses. Fluffy needed a stiff drink, too.

DAD: Never mind about Mrs Simpson and Fluffy. What about Gemma? Just look at the time. That kettle is hissing. I'm going to find this Wayne's phone number and tell his parents just what I think about their son. *(He storms out of the kitchen.)*

MUM: I'd rather you didn't.

(Mum pours cold water in the kettle as a dirty face appears at the window. She grabs a pan to throw.)

MUM: Who is it?! Who's out there?

(A hand taps softly at the back door.)

MUM: You won't get in the door. It's locked. If you're a burglar – Aaah! There's blood!

(Wayne's face presses against the glass. There is blood over his nose.)

WAYNE: It's me. It's Wayne.

MUM: Wayne? What's the matter? Where's Gemma?

WAYNE: She's … upside down in the wheelie bin.

MUM: *(Opening the window)* What's she doing?

WAYNE: Trying to get out. Sorry about this, Mrs Huntley. We've had trouble.

MUM: You'll have more if Dad comes back. Quick, climb in the window. Keep quiet.

WAYNE: Just a nose bleed. A bit of a fight. Sorry we're late. Gemma – let me pull you up.

(He climbs on the window sill as Gran enters.)

GRAN: I'll just get a cuppa before the film. I do wish Bob would stop marching up and down.

MUM: Don't scream.

GRAN: I never scream at horror films. It's called 'The Face At The Window'.

(Gemma appears at the window. She looks a mess, with a cabbage leaf on her head.)

MUM: Try to stay calm.

GRAN: *(She sees them but stays calm)* Would you like a hot drink? You must be chilly out there.

(Jack enters. Gran quickly pulls the curtains across.)

JACK: Any chance of some more pizza?

GEMMA: *(From outside)* Wayne!

JACK: What was that?

GRAN: Me. I said 'rain'. That's why I shut the curtains. It looks like it might rain. Chilly, too.

MUM: The kettle's about to boil. I'll bring you a drink if you go back in the living room.

DAD: *(Bursting in)* Has that kettle boiled?

MUM: *(Acting coolly)* Not yet, dear. Plenty of time.

DAD: Why are those curtains shut?

JACK: Rain.

DAD: What?

JACK: RAIN.

WAYNE: *(Outside)* Yes?

DAD: Who said that?

GRAN: Me, dear. Yes, it is raining. Nasty night.

DAD: All the more reason for her to be home.

JACK: Come on, Gran – our film's starting. *(He goes back into the sitting room.)*

DAD: She's now twenty-five minutes late. It is no joke. I am going to phone that yob's parents. Five minutes, then I'll phone the police. And no one will stop me. *(He storms out.)*

GRAN: *(Opening the curtains)* Quick. In you come. We can't open the door. Dad's got the key.

MUM: What were you doing in the wheelie bin?

GEMMA: I stood on it on the shed to get up to my room.

WAYNE: Sorry about this.

GRAN: Not at all. It's exciting!

MUM: You look a real mess.

GEMMA: Mum, don't tell Dad. He'll go up the wall.

GRAN: He's already up it! Never mind, we'll sort it out. Just get in off that window ledge.

WAYNE: You go first, Gemma. I'll hold your arm. Just put your foot through there.

GEMMA: I'll try. I can't really see. *(She steps into the sink)* Errrr!

MUM: That's the sink. Full of washing up. At least you've got nice clean shoes now!

GEMMA: Ah! My heel is stuck down the plug hole.

GRAN: What fun to be young!

MUM: Hurry up. Dad will be back in a minute.

WAYNE: Anyone got a tissue? My nose bleed is off again.

MUM: Use this kitchen roll. Pop that up your nostril. Now you've got blood on the curtains. I've got drips in my hair, too.

GRAN: *(Singing)* 'Wayne drops keep falling on my head!'

GEMMA: Thanks, Mum. You don't know how great it is to be back home and on solid ground. *(They hug. Wayne grunts.)*

GRAN: I can't hear you with that tissue up your nose, Wayne. Jump down and I'll catch you! Ooh, It's years since a young man leapt at me!

MUM: Quick, someone's coming. Both of you get in the cupboard. *(She bundles them in as Dad enters.)*

DAD: They're engaged.

GRAN: I don't think so, Bob. They're just good friends.

DAD: *(He frowns at Gran)* The phone. I can't get through. I see Gemma's left her mobile on the fridge. Typical. What's that red mark on the curtains?

MUM: *(Quickly)* Beetroot.

GRAN: *(Just as quickly)* Tomato sauce.

DAD: *(Going to the cupboard)* Then you'd better get some bleach from the cupboard…

MUM: *(She shouts in a panic)* No!

GRAN: I'll wash them tomorrow. Don't worry now.

MUM: *(Trying to be calm)* The kettle's boiled. Hot drink?

GRAN: With a spot of brandy? That always calms your nerves, dear.

DAD: Make it a big spot, then. I need it. She's gone too far this time. There's going to be the biggest row of all time when she walks in.

JACK: *(Enters)* Come on, Gran. There's already been three murders. Lots of blood.

DAD: And you're not helping, young man. I'm going to try that phone again. *(He storms out.)*

JACK: What's going on, Mum? Something's fishy.

GRAN: Jack, can you keep a secret?

JACK: For you, Gran, I'll keep anything.

GRAN: I'll treat you to a Big Mac with all the trimmings in town tomorrow.

JACK: What do you want?

GRAN: Just keep quiet about this. *(She opens the cupboard.)*

WAYNE: *(The tissue is still up his nose)* Hi yer, Jack!

GEMMA: Don't you tell Dad, or I'll kill you, Jack.

MUM: He's trying to phone your parents, Wayne.

JACK: Don't worry. I gave him the wrong number.

GRAN: Well done! You'll have a huge coke, as well!

JACK: You look a right mess, Wayne.

GEMMA: He was looking after me! This thug tried to get me to buy a tablet.

WAYNE: I had to defend her to the death!

GEMMA: Wayne was great. He sorted him out. But we missed the last bus.

MUM: Well done, Wayne.

WAYNE: I'd better tell Gemma's dad what happened.

(They all speak at once.)

JACK: You must be joking!

GEMMA: Not tonight.

GRAN: Not wise at the moment.

MUM: Wait till he calms down.

(Pause.)

WAYNE: Won't he be pleased when he hears the truth?

GEMMA: He won't believe us. The thug was Malcolm.

JACK: Oh heck, not Malcolm! The son of Dad's boss. That's done it. Dad will never believe you!

GRAN: *(Holding a bottle)* Don't you worry. Leave it to me. Dad will be fine after a big nightcap! *(She winks and writes on a note pad)* And I've got a plan for Wayne to try.

JACK: Good old Gran. Supergran to the rescue!

MUM: Look out – Dad's coming back.

GRAN: In that case, Jack, it's over to you.

JACK: Me?

GRAN: Yes. Go out there and stop him coming in.

JACK: I'll try – for extra French fries and apple pie!

(He goes out.)

GRAN: Right, back in the cupboard, Wayne.

WAYNE: Back in the cupboard? It's dark in there!

GRAN: It'll be dark everywhere. See that fuse box? We're going to have a blackout. Then give us ten minutes before you call this number on the mobile. *(She gives him a note pad)* This tells you what to do. Now, hurry up and flick that switch!

(Blackout.)

SCENE THREE

The same evening, ten minutes later. The sitting room is dark, lit by a candle. Dad tries to read the phone book. Gran, Mum and Jack sit with coffee. The air is tense.

DAD: I can't see a thing.

GRAN: Have a splash more brandy, Bob.

DAD: I need more than a splash. *(He pours in a lot)* I'm phoning the police. *(He makes the call.)*

JACK: They might send a police car. Cool!

GRAN: Will it have a flashing blue light?

DAD: I hope so. That will give her a shock. *(Talking to the police)* Ah yes, I want to report a missing person … Gemma Huntley.

JACK: *(Whispers)* A boy in my class was fined for that.

MUM: For what?

JACK: For wasting police time. It's a crime.

GRAN: What did he do, Jack?

JACK: He reported his dog was missing – but it was upstairs under his bed all the time.

DAD: *(Still on the phone)* That's right. She's sixteen. She had to be in at eleven and I'm cross … Pardon? No, I am not drunk!

MUM: Bob, I think I need to have a word with you.

DAD: *(Phone)* I want you to find her and give her a good talking to. She's at Tramps nightclub.

(The lights come on.)

GRAN: I knew the power would come back soon.

JACK: Great – now we can watch the TV.

DAD: *(Phone)* No, I can't tell you what she's wearing … No, I can't tell you who she's with – apart from Wayne. I want you to find her. I pay my taxes, you know.

MUM: Oh no. It's all that brandy. He's talking rubbish.

GRAN: You'd better put the cork in the bottle.

DAD: *(Phone)* No, I don't know how tall she is. Er … I'm not sure about her eyes. I think …

(The door opens. Gemma enters. She's in her dressing gown, looking sleepy.)

GEMMA: Green. My eyes are green.

DAD: *(Phone)* She says they're green. *(To Gemma.)* Thanks. *(He does a double take)* What are you doing here?!

GEMMA: There's a lot of noise down here. You woke me up. Have you been drinking, Dad?

DAD: But … *(on the phone)* Don't worry – she's back!

(He slams the phone down.)

GRAN: *(Acting surprised)* Gemma, were you in bed?

MUM: We thought you were still out.

JACK: When did you get back?

GEMMA: Hours ago. I didn't go to the club after all. I felt tired, so I had an early night. I've been here all the time.

DAD: But … You've just made me look a fool.

GRAN: You did that on your own, dear!

GEMMA: I left a note on your chair, Dad. Look, here it is. *(She secretly puts it by his chair)* I thought Jack saw me come in.

JACK: No, I didn't. You'd better hide this note, Dad. The police might use it as proof!

GRAN: They may call you back for a little chat, Bob. After all, you did waste some of their time.

(Wayne calls from the mobile in the kitchen. Dad jumps as his phone rings.)

JACK: They must have traced your number.

DAD: *(He picks up the phone)* Yes?

WAYNE: *(On the kitchen mobile)* Mr Huntley? This is the police. About your daughter …

DAD: *(Phone)* Yes, er … she's right here.

WAYNE: It's a big fine for wasting police time, you know. We're watching you.

DAD: *(Scared)* Very sorry. I was worried about her being with Wayne.

WAYNE: Wayne is a fine lad. We wish more boys were like him. Not like that Malcolm.

DAD: Malcolm? He's a nice young man.

(Gran goes out to the kitchen. She pats Wayne on the back.)

WAYNE: Don't let your daughter go near him. He's bad news. He's into drugs.

DAD: Really, officer? I'm so glad you said. I'll make sure I ask Wayne to come round.

WAYNE: *(He forgets himself)* But I'm here!

DAD: *(Phone)* Pardon?

WAYNE: *(Phone, trying to correct himself)* Er … I said I hear he is a hero. He saved Gemma from trouble tonight.

DAD: That girl is always trouble. I'm about to give her a piece of my mind.

WAYNE: I think you should give her a reward for being so brave. In the fight her dress got torn. She could do with some cash for a new one. Fifty quid would be nice!

DAD: *(Shocked)* Fifty pounds! That's a bit steep.

WAYNE: *(Phone)* Not as steep as the fine we might charge you, sir. I can smell brandy down this phone!

DAD: *(Phone)* What? You think I've been drinking?

WAYNE: We'll be sending someone round to check. Oh, and one more thing, sir…

DAD: Yes, officer?

WAYNE: Don't worry about your daughter staying out late from now on. She's got more sense than you.

DAD: Yes. Yes. Anything you say. *(Slams down phone.)*

GEMMA: Dad, why is your mouth wide open?

DAD: They're going to send someone round.

(Gran comes in from the kitchen. She winks at Jack.)

31

GRAN: There are two policemen at the backdoor, Bob.

GEMMA: You can't talk to them smelling of brandy, dad.

DAD: You talk to them, Doreen.

MUM: You phoned them, you talk to them.

GRAN: They've got handcuffs and tear-gas! *(She winks.)*

DAD: What am I going to say?

GEMMA: Simple. Burst open the door and shout what you always do. Just six words …

JACK: We've heard them every day of our lives …

MUM: For the last fifteen years …

ALL: WHAT TIME DO YOU CALL THIS?!

(Blackout.)